Religions of the World

Islam

David Self

WORLD ALMANAC® LIBRARY

Please visit our web site at: www.worldalmanaclibrary.com
For a free color catalog describing World Almanac® Library's list of high-quality
books and multimedia programs, call 1-800-848-2928 (USA) or 1-800-387-3178
(Canada). World Almanac® Library's fax: (414) 332-3567.

Library of Congress Cataloging-in-Publication Data

Self, David.
    Islam / by David Self.
      p. c.m. — (Religions of the world)
    Includes bibliographical references and index.
    ISBN 0-8368-5868-9 (lib. bdg.)
    ISBN 0-3868-5874-3 (softcover)
    1. Islam—Juvenile literature. 2. Islam—Doctrines—Juvenile literature.
  I. Title. II. Religions of the world (Milwaukee, Wis.)
  BP161.3.S45   2006
  297—dc22   2005041744

This edition first published in 2006 by
World Almanac® Library
330 West Olive Street, Suite 100
Milwaukee, WI 53212 USA

This edition copyright © 2006 by World Almanac® Library. Original edition copyright © 2005 by
Hodder Wayland. First published in 2005 by Hodder Wayland, an imprint of Hodder Children's Books,
a division of Hodder Headline Limited, 338 Euston Road, London NW1 3BH, U.K.

Consultant: Dr. Fatma Amer, The London Central Mosque
Project Editor, Hodder Wayland: Kirsty Hamilton
Editor: Nicola Barber
Designer: Janet McCallum
Picture Researcher: Shelley Noronha, Glass Onion Pictures
Maps and artwork: Peter Bull
World Almanac® Library editor: Gini Holland
World Almanac® Library cover design: Kami Koenig

Photo Credits
The Art Archive/Turkish and Islamic Art Museum Istanbul/Harper Collins Publishers 8; Dagli Orti 31;
Bridgeman Art Library www.bridgeman.co.uk/University Library, Istanbul, Turkey 38; Corbis/SUPRI/
Reuters 44; © John A. Giordano/Corbis: cover; Hutchison Picture Library 29; Impact Photos 4;
Alex Keene 26; Ann and Bury Peerless 12, 39, 41; Peter Sanders Photography Ltd 6, 7, 9, 18, 19, 20,
23, 24, 28, 30, 32, 34, 35, 36, 37, 40; Topfoto 11, 13, 14, 15, 16, 17, 21, 22, 25, 33, 42, 43, 45

Printed in China

1 2 3 4 5 6 7 8 9 09 08 07 06 05

The author acknowledges the help of Abdul Majid Jawad in the writing of the text of this book.

Contents

Note

When Muslims use the name of their Prophet, they usually follow his name with the blessing "Peace be upon him" (often written as pbuh). In this book, that blessing is implied for the faithful, but not written out. In the Western world, years are numbered as either B.C. ("Before Christ") or A.D. ("Anno Domini"—which is Latin for "In the year of our Lord"). In this book, the more neutral terms B.C.E. ("Before the Common Era") and C.E. ("Common Era") are used. The Muslim calendar counts years from the date on which the Prophet and his companions left Mecca for Medina. Its years are numbered A.H. ("After the Hijrah").

Introduction

For Muslims, the followers of the religion Islam, the most important teacher in the world is the Prophet Muhammad. For them, the Prophet Muhammad is the last and the greatest of the prophets of God.

One God

The Prophet Muhammad worked as a trader in the city of Mecca (also known as Makkah) in what is now Saudi Arabia. Muslims believe that an angel appeared to him several times, giving him messages that he was to repeat to the people of Mecca. These messages were later collected together to form the Muslim holy book, the Koran (also known as the Quran or Qur'an). Muslims believe the Koran is the word of God, written in its own style of Arabic. It is always treated with great respect, because it is believed to be the word of God. The most important message, or teaching, of the angel was that there is only one God, whose name is God—or, in Arabic, *Allah*.

Islam

The teaching that the Prophet Muhammad brought to his people is not named after him but is known as Islam, which means "peace and submission" (or "obedience to God"). Nor are the followers of Islam named after him: they are called Muslims.

For Muslims, the Prophet did not start a new religion. He taught the same message as the other prophets of God who had lived before him including Noah, Ibrahim (Abraham), Musa (Moses) and Isa (Jesus): that there is one and only one true God. In Arabic, this teaching is called *tawhid*.

Islam Worldwide

Islam is now the second largest religion in the world, with about 1.3 billion Muslims living in almost every country worldwide.

◄ *In desert countries, people often travel in the cool of the night. The stars are their guide and the moon is their light—so a star and the crescent moon form the symbol of Islam, seen here on a building in the Maldives.*

In more than fifty countries, there are more Muslims than followers of any other religion. These countries stretch from Morocco in northwest Africa across North Africa to the Middle East, and east to Afghanistan and Pakistan. There are also many Muslims in central Africa, as well as in Indonesia, China, and Russia. Many Muslims have settled in European countries—for example, there are about 1.5 million Muslims living in Britain.

For eight hundred years, the Muslim people led the world in providing education and in the development of science. From the eighteenth century C.E. onward, however, many Muslim countries came under Western control, some being conquered by European armies and then ruled as part of Western empires. In the last sixty years, most of these countries have regained their independence, and Muslims are now eager to preserve their own ways of life based on the Koran and the teachings of the Prophet Muhammad.

Countries with the Largest Muslim Populations

Country	Approximate number of Muslims
Indonesia	170,310,000
Pakistan	136,000,000
Bangladesh	106,050,000
India	103,000,000
Turkey	62,410,000
Iran	60,790,000
Egypt	53,730,000
Nigeria	47,720,000
China	37,108,000

▼ In large nations like Russia and India, large numbers of Muslims make up a small percentage of the total population.

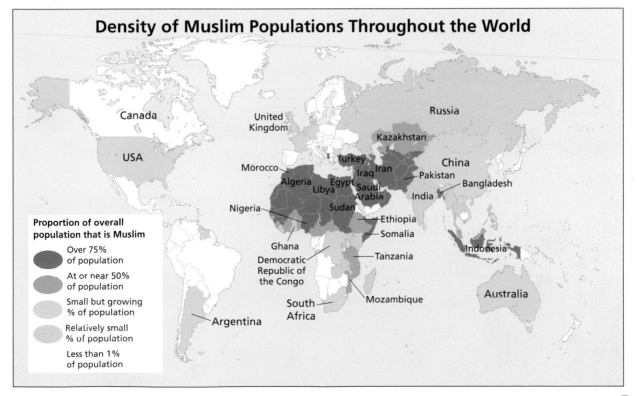

Density of Muslim Populations Throughout the World

Proportion of overall population that is Muslim

- Over 75% of population
- At or near 50% of population
- Small but growing % of population
- Relatively small % of population
- Less than 1% of population

The Growth of Islam

Islam is one of the great religions of the world. It teaches that there is only one God—a God who has made everything, knows everything, and sees everything. As Muslims say, "There is no God but Allah."

The Prophet of Islam

Muhammad lived in the city of Mecca, in what is now Saudi Arabia, from the year 570 C.E. until 632. His father died before his birth and his mother died when he was six, so he was looked after by his grandfather and later by an uncle. His family was quite poor and, like most people at that time, he was not taught to read or write. When he grew up, he worked for his uncle, who was a trader in the city. He soon gained a reputation for exceptional honesty, and many people called him "The Trustworthy." Later, Muhammad worked for a wealthy widow named Khadijah, who also lived in Mecca, helping her manage her business. Eventually Khadijah proposed marriage to him. Muhammad accepted, and Khadijah went on to bear him six children.

▼ *The Great Mosque of Mecca, showing the black, cube-shaped* Kaaba (Ka'bah) *in its courtyard* (see page 9), *and the modern city beyond its walls.*

Mount Hira

At that time, the people of Mecca had forgotten their earlier belief in the one God. Instead of worshiping one God, many people worshiped statues or idols made of stone or wood and were also leading immoral lives. There was much fighting, drinking, and poverty. Although Muhammad was happy and content with his own life, he became increasingly concerned about the social injustices he saw in Mecca. He felt the need to be close to God, and he would often walk north out of Mecca to a hill called Mount Hira. There he sat in a hillside cave. As he watched the stars and the moon, it is said he came to know the greatness of God.

The Angel Jibril

One night, when Muhammad was in the cave, he heard a voice. In front of him he saw a holy spirit, the Angel Jibril (also known as Gabriel). "Recite" said the angel. "What should I recite?" asked Muhammad. "Recite in the name of God." Muhammad repeated the words the angel spoke to him until he knew them by heart.

Ten months later, the angel appeared to him again. "Warn the people. Tell them they must worship and praise the one God and give up their wicked ways." After that, the Angel Jibril appeared often to Muhammad, giving him many more revelations (messages) that he was to teach to the people of Mecca—especially the message that there is only one God, whose name is Allah.

From then on, Muhammad was known as the Prophet and Messenger of God, and all that the angel told him was preserved in the Koran, which is treasured by all Muslims as the word of God.

➤ It is in this cave in the rock face of Mount Hira that the Prophet is said to have prayed before being visited by the Angel Jibril.

Mecca

Some time after the Angel Jibril had revealed the teaching of the Koran to the Prophet, he started to teach the people of Mecca what had been told to him. Many listened and became followers of these teachings, the way of Islam.

There were, however, many people in Mecca who did not welcome the Prophet's new message about the One God. These people worshiped idols and other gods. They thought that if Muhammad persuaded everyone that their idols were worthless and had them destroyed, nobody would visit the city and their businesses would be ruined. The rulers of Mecca tried to starve the Prophet and his family to death by cutting off all his sources of food. When that failed, they tried to stop people from trading with his family. That also failed. After two years, they decided to kill Muhammad while he slept.

The Spider's Web

Muslims believe that God warned the Prophet in a vision of what was about to happen. Under the cover of darkness, Muhammad and his faithful friend and servant, Abu Bakr, managed to escape. Traveling south, they eventually reached some mountains where they found a cave in which to hide.

The Prophet's enemies pursued the fugitives to the mountains. Inside the cave, the Prophet and Abu Bakr heard their enemies approaching. Outside, the trackers found the mouth of the cave. One of the trackers pointed to a spider's web that covered its entrance. Above it, a branch hung low, weighed down by a gray dove that was singing gently. Fooled by the spider's web and the dove, the pursuers moved on, believing that nobody had entered that cave for months.

Al Hijrah

Eventually, the Prophet and Abu Bakr made the difficult journey across the desert to a place called Yathrib, which became known as the city of Medina (also spelled Al Madinah) in present-day Saudi Arabia. Welcomed, the Prophet taught his message in safety. It was in Medina that the first mosque was built.

Eight years later, in the year 630 C.E., the Prophet was able to return in triumph to Mecca, where the people accepted Islam as their religion. All the idols were removed from a holy place called the *Kaaba*, which Muslims believe was the first house built on earth for the worship of the one God.

The Muslim calendar dates from the departure of the Prophet from Mecca (July 16, 622 C.E.) on his journey to Medina. The event is celebrated annually as *Al Hijrah*, which means "the journey" or "migration," and is the first day of the Muslim year.

The Kaaba

The Kaaba is a building shaped like a cube: 39 feet (12 meters) long, 33 feet (10 m) wide, and 49 feet (15 m) high (the word Kaaba means "cube"). Muslims believe the first Kaaba was built by the first man, the biblical Adam, after he had been sent away from the Garden of Eden, as a house in which to praise God. Later, a man Muslims call Ibrahim (and whom Jews and Christians call Abraham) built a new Kaaba in the same place. This Kaaba was kept holy for many years— but was then used for pagan worship until the Prophet Muhammad yet again made it a place for worship to the One God. (See page 30 for more about the Kaaba.)

➤ *Pilgrims in their white robes surround the Kaaba.*

◄ *This painting is a Muslim artist's representation of the building of the Prophet's house, which was also the first mosque, in Medina. The painting dates from the eighteenth century.*

The Muslim Calendar

Islamic years are counted from the Hijrah (A.H. means "After the Hijrah"), which occurred on July 16, 622 C.E. There are roughly 103 Muslim (lunar) years to every 100 Western (solar) years (see page 27). Common Era years (that is, years A.D.) can be calculated using this formula:

C.E. (or A.D.) year = A.H. year + 622 −(A.H. year ÷ 33).

To calculate Islamic years from C.E. (or A.D.) years, use this formula:

$$\text{A.H. year} = \text{C.E. year} -622 + \frac{\text{C.E. year} -622}{32}$$

The Four Caliphs

The Prophet Muhammad died in 632 C.E. After his death, his close friend and son-in-law, Abu Bakr, became the chosen leader of the Muslims and successor to the prophet. The Arabic word for successor is *khalifah*, or caliph. A good and kind man, Abu Bakr ruled for two years until his own death. He was followed by a clever political leader and military general named Umar, who ruled for ten years until he was murdered in 644 C.E.

Before his death, Umar set up a council that would choose the next caliph. The council suggested two men, Uthman bin Affan and Ali bin Talib, both sons-in-law of the Prophet. Eventually Uthman (who was a gentle and a generous man) was elected by the elders of the people as the third caliph. He ruled for ten years until his assassination in 656 C.E.

Ali, who was the Prophet's cousin as well as his son-in-law, became the fourth caliph. He proved to be a brave but humble leader and his many speeches, sermons, and letters are highly regarded. In 661 C.E., he too was murdered.

These first four caliphs are known as the *rashidun*, or "rightly guided"; that is, they were seen as God's representatives on earth. In later centuries, the word *caliph* was also used to mean an (unelected) leader or emperor.

The Spread of Islam

Within one hundred years of the death of the Prophet, Islam had spread far beyond the Arabian peninsula. Muslim armies first marched into nearby countries and then moved rapidly on, conquering as they went. The armies were followed by traders and teachers of the faith. By the year 732 C.E., Muslims ruled from Spain to India, including southern France, all of northern Africa, Egypt, Arabia, and what are now Iraq and Iran. Although there were different rulers in different areas, all were united by the Arabic language and laws based on the Koran.

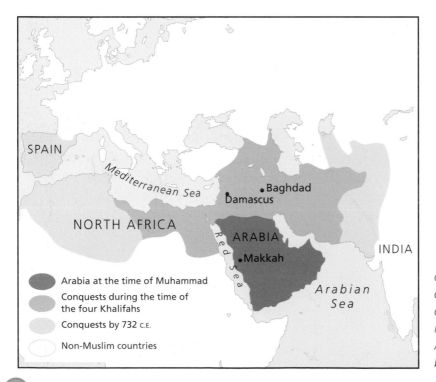

◄ *This map shows the rapid dissemination of Islam after the death of the Prophet. By the time of the caliph Umar, 634 C.E., Muslims ruled from Libya to Afghanistan, as well as in what became known as Arabia.*

Shiite and Sunni

Following the death of the Prophet, there were people who opposed his successors and who wanted Ali (see page 10) to be caliph instead. Those who supported Ali wanted all future leaders to come from the Prophet's family. These supporters became known as the Shi'at-Ali, which means "the party of Ali." They continued to be a strong group within Islam and today they are known as Shiite (Shi'ah) Muslims. Many Shiites believe it is right to fight for what they believe, even if it means being killed themselves. They live mainly in Iran and southern Iraq.

About 90 percent of Muslims belong to a group called the Sunnis, who take their name from the Sunnah *(see page 19), the "way of the Prophet." As do Shiites, Sunni Muslims follow the teachings of the Prophet and believe that the Koran shows them the way to live. They respect Muslim teachers called* imams, *but, unlike the Shiites, the Sunnis do not have any special clergy or priests. Shiites believe there were twelve imams who had special powers, the first imam being Ali, the fourth caliph. They are now led by teachers called* ayatollahs *and have other clergy and teachers who explain hidden meanings in the Koran.*

➤ *Although most Muslims in Pakistan are Sunnis, there are many Shiites. Here they carry black flags at the festival of Ashura (see pages 26 and 27), in memory of the martyrdom of al-Husain ibn Ali, son of the fourth caliph, Ali.*

Jerusalem

Conflict between Islamic and Christian (Western) countries dates from early times. There were especially bitter quarrels about the city of Jerusalem, a holy city for Jews, Christians, and Muslims. The second caliph, Umar, captured Jerusalem in 638 C.E. On entering the city, Umar treated all the people well; it is said that nobody was harmed. Much later, however, in 1071 C.E., the Seljuk Turks conquered the holy lands, persecuted Christians, and prevented Christian pilgrims from visiting Jerusalem and its holy sites. In response, in 1099, Christian armies laid siege to the city and eventually captured it back from Muslim control, reportedly killing 70,000 people during this "crusade." Muslims re-captured the city once again in 1187. Their leader, Salah-ad-Din (sometimes known as Saladin), ordered that no Christian should be harmed and made peace with King Richard I of England. The crusades nonetheless continued through the thirteenth and fourteenth centuries, as Christian armies tried to take Jerusalem back under their control.

➤ *The Dome of the Rock (Qubbat al-Sakhra) in Jerusalem is built on the spot from which the Prophet is said to have been taken on a "Night Journey" to heaven by the Angel Jibril.*

Powerful Empires

All this time, the Muslim world prospered and gained in power and wealth. Many Islamic empires were established, including the mighty Ottoman Empire, which lasted from about 1300 to 1920. Based in what is now Turkey, at one time it stretched from Algeria in North Africa to Basra in Iraq and north to include Hungary and parts of Russia. Its greatest ruler was Emperor Suleiman, who held power in the sixteenth century. His palaces in the Ottoman capital, Istanbul, so dazzled Western visitors that they called him Suleiman the Magnificent. At about the same time, another powerful Muslim empire, that of the Moguls, stretched from Afghanistan to much of India. The Muslim rulers of these great empires were Mogul rulers who claimed descent from warlike tribes in Mongolia, while the Ottoman rulers were Turks. In both empires, the discovery of gunpowder was used to gain and keep power, and the imperial courts were centers of splendor, vast wealth, luxury, and learning.

The Moguls

The mighty Mogul Empire was founded by Babur in 1526. Babur became ruler of Turkestan when he was twelve and later conquered Afghanistan. In 1525, he invaded India and conquered large areas of the country over the next two years. Babur's grandson, Akbar (ruled 1556–1665), doubled the size of the area under Mogul control, so that the Mogul Empire stretched across almost all of what is now India and Pakistan. Akbar built great palaces at Delhi and Agra. The Mogul Empire was attacked by the Persians (now Iranians) in 1739, and during the nineteenth century the British gradually took control of the country, bringing the Mogul Empire to an end in 1858.

➤ This painting of the Mogul court shows two Christian priests visiting the Emperor Akbar. It is from the Akbar-nama, a chronicle of Akbar's reign completed in the late sixteenth century.

Ruled by the West

For 250 years, from about 1700 to 1950, large parts of the Muslim world came under Western rule. It was in 1857, for example, that what had been the great Muslim city of Delhi in India was captured by the British.

Many Muslim countries became colonies in empires ruled by Britain, France, and the Netherlands. In Indonesia, the Dutch did not allow local people to go to secondary school. In Tunisia, the French created laws that made traditional Muslim medicine against the law. In some places, Islamic libraries were destroyed, and treasures were removed and taken back to Western cities.

New Movements

Some Muslims said that the end of the Muslim empires was largely the fault of the Muslims themselves. They suggested that some Muslim emperors had become corrupt and too fond of luxury for themselves and that these rulers had neglected the poor in their own empires. They also said that there had been too many arguments and divisions between Muslim leaders and that religious scholars, eager to preserve their own power, had prevented new ideas from spreading.

Many Muslims began to emphasize the need to re-visit the teachings of the Koran and to live them in their purest form. In the twentieth century, the result of this new emphasis was the start of many Muslim reformation movements, beginning in Arabia, where, in 1926, the Islamic kingdom of Saudi Arabia came into being. Since the end of World War II (in 1945), Muslim countries have regained their independence. For example, in 1947, British rule came to a violent end in India as the country was partitioned, or divided, into two separate countries. In the northwest, the independent state of Pakistan was set up in a region where mainly Muslim people had lived. The larger area, which was mainly Hindu, kept the name of India.

◄ These oil fields in Kuwait help supply fuel to the Western world. It was the invasion of this area by Saddam Hussein of Iraq in 1990 that caused the first Gulf War.

The discovery of oil has brought new wealth to some Muslim countries, particularly in the Middle East. The Islam-majority countries of Saudi Arabia, Iraq, United Arab Emirates, Kuwait, Iran, and Libya are all ranked among the world's top ten oil-producing countries. At the same time, people in some of these countries, such as Iran, have turned against Western values and are trying to lead their lives independent of Western culture and in a way that they feel is faithful to the teachings revealed by the Prophet. In such countries, Islamic sharia (law) rules most legal issues.

▼ *Those Sufis who perform whirling dances have sometimes been known as "whirling dervishes." The Arabic word "dervish" simply means a "member of a religious group."*

Sufis

Since the early days of Islam, there have been Muslims who have tried to become as close to God as possible by leading a very simple way of life. Such people became known as Sufis because they wore long woolen robes, called sufs, of the kind said to be worn by the Prophet Muhammad when he visited the cave at Hira. Sufis use techniques such as chanting or performing rhythmic, whirling dances to try to achieve a closeness with God.

2

Muslim Beliefs and Teachings

For all Muslims, faith is built upon the Koran. The Koran tells Muslims what they should believe and how they should live their lives. Muslims believe that the Koran was not written by the Prophet but is God's own word and therefore should always be treated with great respect.

The Koran

The Prophet Muhammad could neither read nor write. Each time the Angel Jibril revealed more of God's teachings to him on Mount Hira, including the fact that Muhammad was to be the last of God's prophets, Muhammad learned them by heart. Back in Mecca, he repeated them to his friends, who also learned them by heart and wrote them down in various places and on any materials that came to hand—parchment, leather, even pieces of bone. After the Prophet had arrived in Medina, the Angel Jibril revealed more teachings to him.

▼ *These two pages from a seventeenth-century Koran, written in Arabic, are beautifully decorated with patterns and geometric designs. The Koran is never illustrated with pictures of living beings (see page 39).*

Translating the Koran

The Koran is not written in "everyday" Arabic but in its own style. When Muslims go to the mosque, they hear it read in this form of Arabic. Nowadays, millions of Muslims do not speak Arabic, and even modern Arabic speakers do not always understand the Arabic of the Koran. For them, the Koran may be translated into their own language—but Muslims believe that no translation can ever convey exactly what the original means.

Arabic letters are very different from Western ones. Sometimes, different English spellings are used to imitate the sound of an Arabic word—which is why the word "Koran" is sometimes spelled "Qur'an" in English.

▼ *Young Muslim girls in the Philippines learn to recite sections of the Koran by heart.*

After his death, the Prophet's closest friend Abu Bakr wanted to keep all the teachings safe, but it was the third caliph, Uthman, who eventually ordered a man named Zaid ibn Thabit and a team of scribes to collect all that had been revealed. The sayings were written down exactly as the Prophet had dictated them, to form the Koran. Ever since then, the words of the Koran, whether written or printed, have remained unchanged. The term *Koran* is Arabic for "recitation"— because of the angel's first word ("Recite") to the Prophet (*see page 7*).

The Koran contains 114 chapters, which are called *surahs*. Each surah, except surah nine, begins with the words: "In the name of Allah, the compassionate, the merciful." These words are called the *Bismillah*. Muslims say the Bismillah before eating or doing any important job as a way of asking God's blessing. It is said that the Bismillah was written on the wings of the Angel Jibril. The Koran itself is treated with great respect and must only be touched with clean hands and never while eating or drinking. It must never touch the ground.

The Teachings of Islam

Muslims respect the holy books of the Jewish religion and the Christian Gospels, but they believe that the Koran is God's final and complete teaching for his people. It is not a book of stories about ancient times—it is a book of teachings, laws, and wise sayings. It is written in a mixture of rhythmic prose and poetry, and its 114 chapters or surahs are always arranged in the same order. It is said that the Angel Jibril told the Prophet that they should be arranged in this way.

The shorter surahs were mostly revealed in Mecca, before the Muslims' migration to Medina. Nearly all of what was revealed in Mecca teaches Muslims about the oneness of God, about creation, and about life after death. These surahs also speak of the greatness and mercy of God.

▼ In accordance with Muslim tradition, these young female students at the Yusuf Islam School in London are wearing head scarves and modest dress.

As a result of the Angel Jibril's instruction, the longer surahs come at the beginning of the Koran. These longer surahs were revealed in Medina after the migration and the establishment of the first Muslim state. That is why they tell Muslims how to live their lives based on equality and social justice. They include laws about how to run the state as well as instructions to dress modestly and to not be greedy. There are rules forbidding Muslims to charge or to pay interest on money that they lend or borrow, and there are instructions to those who act as judges that they should always be merciful.

The Sirah

It is said that everything the Prophet Muhammad did was written down so that Muslims know how he spoke, slept, dressed, and walked. They know about his behavior as a husband and a father and how he treated women, children, and animals. Taken together, these writings are called the Sirah.

▲ *Two Muslim boys enjoy Koran school in the Islamic Republic of Mauritania, in western Africa. Even though they speak Hansaniya Arabic, they learn the extracts from the Koran on their tablets in traditional Arabic.*

The Hadith

Some years after the death of the Prophet, all his sayings were collected together. Scholars had strict rules for deciding which sayings were to be included, and those sayings that were agreed upon as being genuine were called the Hadith, which means "statement."

The Sunnah

Together, the Sirah and the Hadith are called the Sunnah. The word means "method" or "example." Muslims try to live their lives in the way shown by the Koran and the Sunnah.

Some Sayings of the Prophet

"The world is green and beautiful and God has made you his steward over it."

"When you go to visit the sick, comfort them in their grief by saying 'You will get well and live long.'"

"God does not look upon your bodies and appearances. He looks upon your hearts and deeds."

"God is gentle and loves gentleness in all things."

The Shahadah

Muslims all around the world learn that the first duty of Islam is to make a statement of their faith. By saying this (and believing it) a person becomes a Muslim. Making a statement of faith is done by reciting the *Shahadah*:

"There is no god but God and Muhammad, peace be upon him, is his Prophet." In Arabic this statement reads as follows: "*La ila' ha illallah Muhammad ur rasulullah.*"

Although Muslims honor and respect other prophets, such as Musa (Moses) and Isa (Jesus), they do not believe that Jesus was divine (that he was the son of God) even though they do believe in his virgin birth. They believe that with Muhammad, God completed the revelation of his truth, a revelation that had begun with the earlier prophets or messengers.

Learning the Koran

Muslims believe that the Koran is the most important book in the world, and many Muslims learn large sections of the Koran by heart, especially when they are young. Schools in many Muslim countries make this a part of the curriculum. In non-Muslim countries, children often go to special classes (sometimes called "mosque school") after their ordinary school day has finished. In these classes, they are taught by the local imam to recite sections of the Koran. The language and the rhythms in which it is written make it easier to learn by heart.

A number of Muslims learn to recite the whole Koran. Anyone who achieves this is much respected and is allowed to use the title *hafiz* as part of his or her name. It is estimated that there are several million people alive at any one time who are hafiz.

▼ As with all Arabic, the Shahadah is read from right to left; one place it is displayed is on the flag of Saudi Arabia.

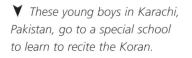
The "Five Pillars" of Islam

Islam has five rules, or "pillars." They are called pillars because they help a Muslim live a good life— in the same way that pillars support a building. They are mentioned throughout the Koran:

1. Shahadah *or making a statement of faith.*

2. Salah *or prayer (see pages 22–23)*

3. Zakah *or helping the needy (see pages 36–37)*

4. Sawm *or fasting (see page 28)*

5. Hajj *or pilgrimage (see pages 30-31)*

Other rules in the Koran teach Muslims always to be honest and generous, never to eat pork or drink alcohol, and never to gamble or lend money for profit. Muslims must also be ready to fight to defend their faith.

▼ *These young boys in Karachi, Pakistan, go to a special school to learn to recite the Koran.*

3

Private and Public Worship

Muslims believe that their whole lives should be lived for God. To be a Muslim is to submit oneself to God, who is merciful and just. Prayer is seen as an act of submission to God.

◄ *A Muslim in Thata, Pakistan, performs the ritual act of* wudu *before prayer. This ritual involves washing first the face, then the hands and lower arms, before washing the feet.*

Salah

One of the five duties of Islam is prayer, which is known as salah (or salat). The Muslim holy book, the Koran, repeatedly says how important it is to pray—and to pray at set times: "Prayer at fixed times has been enjoined on the believers."

Muslims pray five times a day at the times taught by the Prophet. These five set times are:

- between the first sign of daylight and sunrise
- just after midday
- just after the middle of the afternoon
- after sunset but before dark
- when it is dark.

These prayers may be said in a mosque or at home, but Muslims can pray anywhere that is clean—provided they have also made themselves clean. This special act of washing before prayer is called *wudu*.

To pray, Muslims must face in the direction of the holy city of Mecca where the Kaaba is (*see page 9*). When they are ready, they often put down a prayer mat before they say their prayers—in Arabic.

A different position is taken for each part of the prayer. First, Muslims stand to show they are listening to God. Then they bow to show respect to God. Next, they bow low twice, touching the ground with forehead, knees, nose, and palms—showing that they are submitting themselves to the will of God. Between each of these low bows, they sit back on their heels. Special words are said at each point, and all the movements are repeated two, three, or four times, according to the time of day. Muslims also say their own private prayers in their own language.

The Exordium

As part of their prayers, Muslims repeat the opening words of the Koran:

"In the name of God,
The most Gracious,
The most Merciful,
All praise be to God alone, the Lord of Creation,
The most Gracious, the most Merciful King of Judgment Day!
You alone we worship and to You alone we pray for help.
Guide us in the right way—the way of those you have blessed, not the way of those that have been condemned by you or of those who go astray.'
—Surah 1

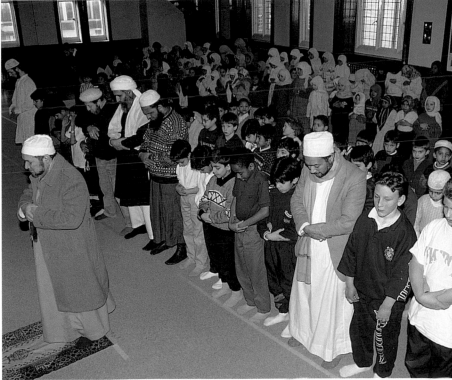

➤ Muslims join in prayer at the Islamia School in Brent, in north London, England.

Going to the Mosque

The place where Muslims gather together to worship God is called a mosque. Many mosques have a tall tower called a minaret. Five times a day, at the set times, a man called a *muezzin* (sometimes spelled *mu'adhin*) traditionally calls Muslims from the minaret to pray to God. The most important prayers of the week are those said after noon on Fridays. At this time, Muslim men go to a mosque to pray together. Women may also go, but many choose to pray at home.

In each mosque, there is a place where Muslims may wash so that they are not dirty in any way when they pray to God. They also take off their shoes before entering a mosque, making sure that the dirty soles of the shoes are not left pointing upward toward God. There are no chairs or seats in the main prayer hall. Often there are mats on which

Muslims can kneel and bow low or "prostrate" themselves to pray. (The word *mosque* means "place for prostration.")

Wherever they are in the world, Muslims face the holy city of Mecca to pray and so, in each mosque, on one wall is an empty arch (called a *mihrab*) that shows the direction of Mecca (the *qiblah*). The person leading the prayers may stand in front of the mihrab.

Although Muslims can worship anywhere that is clean, the Koran says that whenever forty men live in the same area, they should have a mosque. Many mosques are large, handsome buildings, often with huge domes, but a mosque may simply be a conversion of an ordinary house. There are never any

▼ The New Federal Mosque in Kuala Lumpur, Malaysia, has a huge central courtyard and two minarets from which the faithful are called to prayer. It was opened in 2000 and can hold up to 17,000 worshipers.

pictures or statues in a mosque. This is because the Prophet Muhammad thought people might worship them instead of God. There are often, however, many beautiful carpets or hangings decorated with patterns or words from the Koran.

In addition to the main area (called the Prayer Hall or Room), there may be a separate area where women can pray. There may also be a courtyard and rooms used for teaching and meetings, but there is no obligation on Muslim women to attend the mosque—and most don't. Instead, they fulfill their daily obligations to pray within the home.

Knowledge

The Prophet once said that it was the duty of every Muslim, male or female, to seek knowledge "even as far away as China." This pursuit to learn new things and to develop new inventions is known as *ilm*. It was once the main driving force of Muslim society, and Muslims started the first universities, public libraries, and public hospitals. The oldest university in the world opened in Cairo, Egypt, in 970 C.E. Some Muslims, however, have interpreted ilm to mean only religious knowledge. When scholars have devoted themselves solely to this "correct" interpretation of scripture, there has been a decline in scientific advance and in independent thought.

The Imam

At Friday prayers, there is a sermon or talk. This is usually given by the imam, a leader or teacher chosen by the other Muslims at that mosque because of his wisdom and knowledge of the Koran.

➤ *Muslim men face the direction of Mecca in the Islamic Cultural Center mosque in New York.*

Festivals and Holy Days

Muslims are required by Islamic law to celebrate at least two festivals: *Id-ul-Fitr* and *Id-ul-Adha*. *Id*, sometimes spelled "Eid," means "festival" (*see page 28*). Many Muslims also celebrate several other special days in each year. The Muslim year is shorter than the Western year (*see box*), so these annual events in the Muslim calendar happen on different dates in the Western calendar every year.

Al Hijrah (1 *Muharram*)

This festival, which occurs on New Year's Day in the Islamic calendar, is a reminder of the Hijrah, when the Prophet Muhammad, traveling with a company of seventy people, migrated from Mecca to Medina in 622 C.E. It was in Medina that he gathered a tribe of followers who accepted him as the last Prophet and began to follow his teachings. The Hijrah marks the start of the spread of Islam around the world (*see page 8*).

Ashura (10 *Muharram*)

On this day, Shiite (Shi'ah) Muslims remember the martyrdom of al-Husain ibn Ali, a grandson of the Prophet, in 680 C.E., at Karbala in Iraq.

Maulid al-Nabi (The Day of the Prophet; 12 *Rabi' al-Awwal*)

The "Day of the Prophet" commemorates both his birth and death.

Laylat-al-Mi'raj (The Night Journey; 27 *Rajab*)

This festival celebrates the "Night Journey" made by the Prophet Muhammad with the Angel Jibril. According to the story, they went from Mecca to Jerusalem in a single night on a winged horse. From a place in Jerusalem where the Dome of the Rock now stands, it is said that the Prophet ascended into heaven to meet the earlier prophets and eventually God. On this night the Prophet learned the importance of praying five times a day. Some Muslims believe that this was not an actual journey but a vision.

Ramadan

Ramadan is the month in which Muslims fast each day during the hours of daylight (*see pages 28–29*).

Laylat-ul-Qadr (The Night of Power; 27 *Ramadan*)

This festival marks the night in which the Koran was first revealed to the Prophet by the Angel Jibril. Many Muslims spend the night reading the Koran or praying in their local mosque.

◄ *A selection of Id (or Eid) cards which Muslims exchange in celebration of the end of the month of Ramadan.*

The Islamic Months

Islam has its own calendar based on the movements of the moon (rather than the movement of the earth around the sun on which the Western calendar is based). This Islamic calendar has twelve months of twenty-nine or thirty days long (the time between one new moon and the next). As a result, Muslim years are usually eleven days shorter than Western years. This means that, each year, Muslim holy days "move" forward through the calendar used in Western countries. Islamic months begin at sunset with the first sighting of the new moon in a given area.

Islamic Months	Festivals *(with date)*
Muharram	1 Al Hijrah *(Prophet's Journey to Medina)*
	10 Ashura
Safar	
Rabi' al-Awwal *(sometimes called* **Rabi I***)*	12 Maulid al-Nabi *(The Day of the Prophet)*
Rabi' ath-Thani *(sometimes called* **Rabi II***)*	
Jamadi al-Awwal *(sometimes called* **Jamadi I** *or* Jumad I*)*	
Jamadi al-Akhir *al- (sometimes called* **Jamadi II** *or* **Jumad II***)*	
Rajab	27 Laylat-al-Mi'raj *(The Night Journey)*
Sha'ban	
Ramadan	27 Laylat-ul-Qadr *(The Night of Power)*
Shawwal	1 Id-ul-Fitr *(The Day after Ramadan)*
Dhul-Qa'da	
Dhul-Hijja	Al Hajj *(The Pilgrimage to Mecca)*
	10 Id-ul-Adha *(End of the Hajj)*

Id-ul-Fitr (1 Shawwal)

The day after Ramadan is a great celebration. In Islamic countries it is a public holiday. It begins with an early meal. Then everyone puts on their best clothes and goes to the mosque, and later they visit relatives and friends to exchange presents and give each other sweets. People wish each other "*Id Mubarak*" ("Blessed be your celebration") and give one another Id cards.

Id-ul-Adha (10 Dhul-Hijja)

This important festival marks the end of the Hajj (*see pages 30–31*). It is celebrated by all Muslims and not just those who make the pilgrimage. An animal (a sheep, goat, cow, or even a camel) is sacrificed, and its meat is shared between the family, friends, and the poor. This is done in remembrance of the sacrifice sent by God to Ibrahim (Abraham) to take the place of Ibrahim's son, whom Ibrahim was about to sacrifice to God.

▲ A British Muslim family share their evening meal after their daily fast during the month of Ramadan.

Ramadan

Ramadan is the ninth month of the Muslim year (*see page 27*) and is special because it was the month in which the Prophet began to receive the teaching of Islam from the Angel Jibril (*see page 7*). To remind themselves of this, Muslims fast on each of the thirty days of Ramadan during daylight hours. They don't eat, drink, or smoke from dawn until sunset. They also avoid all sexual relations at this time. Fasting (*sawm*) is one of the five rules or "pillars" of Islam that Muslims must obey (*see page 21*).

The month begins with the first sighting of the new moon, so the fast starts at slightly different times in different countries. During this month, Muslims are also meant to say extra prayers and to try to read the whole of the Koran. All adult Muslims are expected to keep the fast, but very old people, people who are ill, those making a long journey, and women who are pregnant or feeding a baby are excused. So too are young children, but most children try to fast once they reach the age of twelve. Some younger ones will fast for part of the day or on Fridays through Sundays to practice. Ramadan is also a time to give to charity.

During the month of Ramadan, before sunrise, Muslims have a meal called *suhoor*, which consists of foods such as bread with olive oil, rice or porridge, boiled eggs, or dates and other fruit. After sunset, they end that day's fast with *iftar*: a few dates or nuts, savory pastries, and fruit drinks. After evening prayers, they share in the main family meal.

In Our Own Words

"I fast not because food is bad or eating is wicked. I fast because going without food all day makes me really enjoy my evening meal. A meal at the end of the day's fast is something I really look forward to. I also fast to remind me that many people are too poor to eat whenever they feel like it. It makes me think of people who live where there's a shortage of food. Often, we reach for something to nibble the moment we feel the slightest bit hungry. Fasting makes me not give in the moment I feel hungry. It helps make my mind stronger than my body."

▼ *In Jakarta, Indonesia, Muslims gather for early morning prayers on Id-ul-Fitr, the day after Ramadan.*

The Kaaba

The fifth duty, or pillar, of Islam is to make a pilgrimage to Mecca. The word for this duty is *Hajj*.

The city of Mecca (in what is now Saudi Arabia) is important to Muslims not only because it was the birthplace of the Prophet of Islam, Muhammad, but also because it is the site of the Kaaba. When Muslims make the Hajj, they believe they are following not only in the footsteps of the Prophet but also in those of Adam and of Ibrahim, whom they consider to be their forefathers (*see page 4*). Today, the Kaaba stands in the courtyard of the Great Mosque of Mecca. It is covered in a black silk and cotton cloth with the words of the Koran embroidered upon it. Inside, the Kaaba is unfurnished. Ordinary pilgrims do not enter it.

Al Hajj

The Hajj is performed during the second week of the twelfth month of the Muslim year. As the pilgrims approach Mecca, they stop to put on pilgrim dress. For a man, this is two pieces of white, unsewn cloth. Women veil their faces. The purpose of this clothing is to stress simplicity and equality: nobody's wealth or status can be told from their dress.

On entering the courtyard of the Great Mosque, pilgrims walk seven times around the Kaaba (which they have always faced when saying their prayers back at home). From the Kaaba, they walk briskly between the two small hills of Safa and Marwah, which are at a close distance from the Kaaba within Mecca. This is done in memory of the

▼ *During the Hajj, pilgrims live in a vast tented city near Mecca.*

time when Hagar, mother of Ishmael (said to be an ancestor of all Muslims—as Ibrahim's other son, Isaac, born to his wife Sarah, is said to be an ancestor of the Jews) searched in this desert place for water for her baby son. It is said that God caused a spring (called Zam Zam) to gush out of the rocky ground. Pilgrims take home water from the spring to those who didn't manage to make the Hajj.

The most important part of the Hajj is when pilgrims travel to the nearby Plain of Arafat, where the Prophet Muhammad preached his last sermon. Here the pilgrims stand and pray in the heat from noon till sunset, asking God for forgiveness. Next they go back toward Mecca, stopping at a place called Mina. Here they perform a ritual "stoning of the devils." Seven stones are thrown at three pillars in memory of how Ibrahim once rejected the devil. An animal is sacrificed and male pilgrims have their heads shaved. All the pilgrims then return to Mecca to perform a further seven circuits of the Kaaba.

▼ *A Muslim who has completed the Hajj is known as "Hajji." This home, in the village of El-Asasif in Egypt, has been decorated to show that its owner is a Hajji.*

4

Living the Faith

Being Muslim is not just about saying prayers, going to the mosque, and feasting or fasting at special times. Being Muslim is a complete way of life—from birth to death. The Koran and the teachings of the Prophet tell a Muslim how to live each minute of each day.

◀ A father whispers the Shahadah into the ear of his new-born baby.

Family Life

For Muslims, the family is all-important. When Muslims become parents, they have a duty to see their children grow up understanding the faith. As soon as a baby is born, its father whispers into its ear the Shahadah: "There is no god but God, and Muhammad, peace be upon him, is his Prophet." In this way, the very first words the baby hears are about God and his Prophet. By hearing these words, the baby is welcomed into the faith. Naming a baby is also important. Sometimes the name of the Prophet or of one of his family is chosen, along with several family names.

Muslim children learn about their religion by watching their parents and following their example—seeing, for instance, how they pray five times a day. Although

Muslims may say these prayers wherever they are, the Prophet told his followers that they should say some of their prayers at home every day.

Muslim children are expected to work hard at school and to help with chores at home. There are rules to guide Muslims when it comes to making friends and spending time outdoors. All teenagers are expected to show respect to older people, because elders have more experience of life than the young. Once grown up, children are expected to care for their parents as they reach old age in return for the care the children received when young. Muslims often live in large family groups, and members of the whole family are expected to help each other at all times.

Family life is so important for Muslims that much of the home may be kept private from outsiders. In addition, males and females usually receive guests separately. Male visitors will be shown to a guest room and will meet the men (and boys) of the family. The women (and girls) may stay in another room, where they may receive their female guests. If a female has a male visitor, male family members will join her to receive him.

Muslims also believe that all believers belong to the one family of Islam, whatever their skin color, and that they should help those members of that family who are poorer than themselves by giving *zakah* (*see page 36*). Helping people may also take forms other than financial help.

▼ *A Muslim family in Hievlev, Denmark, come together to celebrate the end of Ramadan—the festival of Id-ul-Fitr (see page 28). Such family occasions are very important times in the Muslim year.*

Marriage

Marriage is very important to Muslims. To be regarded as a fully grown-up member of the family, a Muslim must usually be married. The Koran encourages all Muslims to marry and to have children.

In Arabia at the time of the Prophet, a man could have as many wives as he chose. The Koran changed this, saying that a man should have no more than four wives. If he did, it was his duty to treat them all equally. It has always been rare, however, for a Muslim man to have more than one wife—partly because very few men could afford to support two wives. Some Muslim men do marry a second wife if the first wife is unable to have children or if she becomes too ill to look after the children. In Western countries, it is against the law for a Muslim to have more than one wife.

Before a Muslim wedding takes place, the couple agree on rules for their marriage, and these rules are written down, signed, and witnessed as a contract between them. There is usually a wedding party about the time the couple begin to live together.

Divorce

Divorce is discouraged but is not forbidden by Islam if the marriage has completely failed. Women as well as men may initiate divorce if they are mistreated or unsupported by their husbands. Laws vary by country, but according to Islamic law, if divorce does happen, the wife receives some money from her ex-husband and keeps all their household goods. The husband then has no more responsibility to her. Re-marriage is allowed.

◄ In Pakistan, a Muslim man and woman (wearing traditional dress) have become husband and wife in the presence of both families. Music and feasting will follow for the rest of the day and long into the night.

Arranged Marriages

For Muslims, a marriage means the joining not just of two people but of two families. For this reason, the choice of partner is seen as a matter of importance to the whole family, and so Muslim marriages are often "arranged" by parents and older relatives. It is often said that parents can see more clearly who would make a good life-long partner for their child than the young person. Most young Muslims are happy to follow their family's choice—but in the twenty-first century, some young Muslims (especially those living in Western countries) want the right to make their own choices. Even where a wedding is "arranged," young people have the right to refuse the person chosen to be their partner. Islamic law forbids forced marriages.

◄ Not every Muslim couple wears traditional dress for their marriage ceremony. In fact, "traditional dress," including head scarves and veils, is guided by local culture as well as Islam, and varies from country to country. This Chinese couple have just married in Mongolia.

Zakah

Zakah (sometimes spelled zakat) is one of the five "pillars" of Islam (*see page 21*). It is the duty or obligation for all those who can afford it to give money or food to the poor and others in need. For example, money may be given to help those who have suffered from a disaster such as an earthquake, or to help with the building of a hospital or mosque —or to help a poor student to study at a college or university.

Zakah is not something a Muslim chooses to do because he or she feels kind or generous—nor is it a tax. Muslims believe that, because everything in the world belongs to God, everything one owns really belongs to God. They also believe that God will judge how wisely each Muslim uses what he or she has been given. Giving "-kah" reminds Muslims of this teaching.

There are complicated rules about how much zakah should be paid. Crops, herds of animals, and deposits in banks all count as part of a person's wealth. Homes, clothes, and furniture do not. It is up to each Muslim to decide if he or she should pay more zakah than necessary, but a minimum of 2.5 percent is required. The percentage owed can vary by

▼ *At a mosque in Buckinghamshire, England, two elders figure out how the zakah should be distributed. In the center is the imam of the mosque.*

▲ *Women in Fes, Morocco, meet together to learn and study the meaning of the Koran.*

a number of factors. For example, while 2.5 percent is generally appropriate for assets acquired in the past year, 5 percent could be owed for the crop that a farmer grows and irrigates (waters) himself, but 10 percent could be owed for the same crop if it is watered by rain alone (at less cost to the farmer). Zakah is usually collected each year at the festival of Id-ul-Fitr and is paid by women and children as well as men—if they have enough wealth. The word *zakah* means "that which makes pure." Zakah is often understood by Muslims as form of worship, a way to purify themselves and their belongings.

The Rich Man and the Poor Man

Besides the religious duty of paying zakah, Muslims are also taught to be generous— as this story or parable shows:

There was once a rich man and a poor man who owed him money. "Sir, I can't pay you what I owe," said the poor man, "but, if you give me time, I'll pay you when I can."

"Very well. Pay me when you can," replied the rich man."

Islam teaches that this rich man will be rewarded by God for being kind. The story goes on, however, to show how much better it might have been:

"Sir, I can't pay you what I owe," said the poor man, "but, if you give me time, I'll pay you when I can."

"You keep what little money you have," replied the rich man. "Forget what you owe me: it will be my zakah."

Knowledge

The Prophet once said that it was the duty of every Muslim, male or female, to seek knowledge "even as far away as China." This pursuit to learn new things and to develop new inventions is known as *ilm*. It was once the main driving force of Muslim society, and Muslims started the first universities, public libraries, and public hospitals. The oldest university in the world opened in Cairo in Egypt in 970 C.E. Some Muslims, however, have interpreted ilm to mean only religious knowledge. When scholars have devoted themselves solely to the "correct" interpretation of scripture, there has been a decline in scientific advance and in independent thought.

Mathematics

What are usually called Arabic numerals (1, 2, 3, and so on) originally came from India, where they were developed by Hindu scholars along with the concept and symbol for zero. It was Muslim mathematicians, however, who first invented decimals and developed the way we do basic arithmetic. Gradually, this system was passed on to the Western world, which, until then, had used Roman numbers (I, II, III, IV, and so on), which are more awkward to use in calculations. Not only did the West begin to use Arabic numerals, it also copied the Arabic system of reading or working traditional addition and subtraction sums from right to left (Arabic writing is read from right to left, as is Hebrew). Muslim scholars invented essential branches of mathematics such as algebra, geometry, and trigonometry, as well as bringing the number zero into use in mathematics.

◄ *This sixteenth-century painting shows Ottoman astronomers at the Galata observatory in Turkey, as they calculate the dimensions of the universe and the movements of the planets.*

Science

Five hundred years before the Western world realized that the earth orbits the sun, Muslim astronomer al-Biruni (973–1048) calculated the time it takes the earth to do so. He also figured out that the earth rotates once a day and discovered the specific gravity of various metals. One of the greatest Muslim scientists, al-Razi (died 925), established midwifery and studied and wrote about eye disorders, measles, and smallpox. Another Muslim scientist, Ibn Sina, also called Avicenna (980–1037), wrote a twenty-four-volume medical encyclopedia that became the standard medical reference in both the Islamic and Western worlds for the next 700 years. The Muslim world developed the science of optics, oils for healing, veterinary science, town planning, and underground mining. Muslim scholars also invented the compass, test tubes, surgical instruments, water mills, windmills—and the guitar.

Art

The Prophet taught that worshiping statues or idols is wrong, so the representation of living beings is strictly forbidden in mosques, in other religious buildings, and in holy books such as the Koran. Muslim artists therefore became experts in the creation of wonderful and intricate designs using flowers, plants, and geometrical patterns. These decorate the walls of mosques and other buildings the world over.

The skill of beautiful handwriting (known as calligraphy) is considered by Muslims to be the greatest form of art, because it is used to write out words from the Koran. Arabic is a flowing, lovely script, and so words from the Koran in beautiful calligraphy have often been used as a surface decoration on the walls of mosques, on tiles, or on decorated pottery. Beautifully patterned cloth, decorated pottery (ceramics), metalwork, glass cutting, and carving are all important forms of art in the Islamic world.

▼ *The walls of the Wazir Khan mosque in Lahore, Pakistan, are covered with decorated tilework, using geometric and floral patterns as well as beautiful calligraphy.*

Death

Muslims try to ensure that nobody dies alone. When someone is dying, family and friends gather around and ask for forgiveness for any harm they have done. If possible, the dying person is reminded of the Shahadah (*see page 20*)—so the person dies as a believer. When death finally happens, the eyes of the dead person are closed, and the body is washed by the family (a man's body by the men, a woman's by the women) and is then wrapped in white sheets. The body of a person who has died in battle is not washed.

In Muslim tradition, burial takes place on or as near to the day of death as possible. The body is taken on a stretcher to the mosque or straight to the burial place, where prayers may be said by an imam. Burial is usually without a coffin so that the body will be in contact with the earth in which it is buried. The head is turned to face Mecca. Women do not usually attend the funeral but visit the grave later. Muslims are never cremated.

Judgment

Islam teaches that each soul has its own separate identity. Muslims do not believe in reincarnation but in a "Day of Judgment" when God will bring everyone back to life and decide how good or bad each person has been. If the good things people have done are greater than the bad things, then an angel will lead them to Paradise. If the bad things are greater, then they will go to hell. Muslims also believe that God is kind and merciful and that he will wipe out the bad things—provided people are truly sorry for what they have done.

➤ This sixteenth-century illustration shows the Mogul emperor Babur instructing his workmen about the planning of a new garden. The Koran says that Paradise is like a perfect garden, a place of peace and happiness. Many Muslim rulers have tried to design gardens similar to the ones in Paradise as described in the Koran.

◄ A Muslim cemetery in Singapore. All Muslims are buried facing Mecca.

In Our Own Words

"When I die, I will be buried. Then the angels will ask me three questions: 'Do I believe in God, do I accept Muhammad as his Prophet, and what is your book?' If I answer correctly, then I will wait until the Day of Judgment. As that's a long time, I'll be told my likely result on that day—whether I'll be going to Paradise or Hell."

5

Islam Today

In the twenty-first century, Islam is seen by some people as being at war with the Western world and set against all the changes in modern life. Muslims themselves are divided as to whether Islam needs to become more "modern," as are some Gulf states such as Kuwait, which is comparatively Westernized. In other countries (such as Saudi Arabia and Iran), Muslim tradition is strictly upheld.

Women in Islam

Islam teaches that men and women are equal but different. For example, politics is usually thought of as a job for men, while women must be responsible for the home and the family. Women, however, have equal rights to own property and to be educated. They are allowed to take jobs outside the home—often working as teachers or in hospitals. This freedom varies from country to country. In Pakistan, for example, a woman became Prime Minister, whereas in other Muslim countries, women are still not allowed to drive cars. Many Muslims now think that women have not always had the dignity that the Koran teaches and have been denied their rights.

Dress

The Koran teaches that both "men and women should lower their gaze and be mindful of their chastity" (Surah 24:30-31). This teaching implies that they should dress modestly. While men usually keep themselves covered at least from the navel to the knees, this rule has often been taken to mean that women must be covered from head to foot, showing only their wrists, feet, and face—and, in some cases, only their eyes. In an extreme example, under the Taliban's control of Afghanistan from 1996–2001, Muslim women were required to wear a *burka,* a narrow cloak that encases the body from head to toe, with only a screened opening for the eyes. In many Muslim countries, strict dress codes are being questioned by some women who increasingly want greater freedom. Others feel that traditional coverings honor their faith.

◄ *Benazir Bhutto was elected Prime Minister of Pakistan in 1988. She was the first female leader of a Muslim state.*

The Hijab

The hijab *is a veil that covers the head and shoulders. It is worn by some Muslim women, but not by others. Here, four Muslim women explain their choice:*

"People think I'm forced to wear the hijab by my parents. I'm not. I want to wear it. It's a benefit. I have more confidence in myself. And people don't swear at me when I'm wearing it."

"We don't wear the hijab all the time. We don't wear it at home when there are just family members around. This is what the Koran says."

"The hijab frees you from everyone brainwashing you, you know, saying 'Buy this, buy that, you're supposed to look like this.' I don't have to worry about being popular by buying things that are 'cool.'"

"I was born in Britain and I've just started working in a bank. I'm allowed to wear the hijab at work but I choose not to. I like the freedom and the chance to dress like the other girls at work."

▼ *Turkey is a secular state in which the vast proportion of the population is Muslim. Some of the women in these groups gathered on the seashore in Istanbul wear the hijab; others wear Western dress.*

Conflict

On September 11, 2001, terrorists hijacked four planes and crashed two of them into the World Trade Center buildings in New York, destroying the buildings and killing nearly three thousand people. A third plane crashed into the Pentagon in Washington, D.C., killing over one hundred more. The terrorists in the fourth plane were overcome by passengers determined to abort another planned attack, and the plane crash-landed in Pennsylvania, killing all on board. The terrorists were Muslims working for Al Qaeda, a militant Islamic terrorist group. Since then, Islam and terrorism have often been linked. As one Muslim said, however, "Those men were senseless. What they did was evil and very wrong. Islam was not to blame."

Islam teaches decency and care for all that God has created. It teaches that violence is wrong and that it is wrong to hurt the innocent. It also, however, teaches that it is right to defend the faith when attacked— but only in self-defense.

Fundamentalism

Fundamentalists are people who believe that holy books (such as the Koran) are true in every word, cannot be altered, and are true today in the same way that they were when they were first written down. Fundamentalists often choose one part of a holy book and concentrate on that, forgetting other things written elsewhere in the book.

In the last thirty years, a number of Muslims have become very angry about what they believe is going wrong in the world, including Western cultural dominance. The result has been the rise of a modern fundamentalism: a desire to strengthen Islam by insisting on the "purest" form of the religion. In practice, Muslim fundamentalism varies from country to country. In Iran, women may drive cars and go out to work, but under the fundamentalist Taliban regime in Afghanistan, women did not even have the right to a basic education or the right to work. The aims of fundamentalists also vary. The militant Palestinian group Hamas wants to create an Islamic republic in just one country. The leader of Al Qaeda, Osama bin Laden, has expressed a desire for a united Islamic empire under central control. These ambitions may be political, but the movements are underpinned by support from religious fundamentalists.

◄ *A woman holds posters reading "Implement sharia law" during a demonstration in Jakarta, Indonesia, in February 2004. The word* sharia *(syariah or shari'ah) means the "way" or "path" to be followed by all Muslims. It has also come to mean "a system of laws" to help Muslims follow this path and is often used to describe the strict legal system in fundamentalist Muslim states.*

▲ In many places around the world, members of the different world faiths meet and work together to try to understand one another better. Here, Christians, Jews, and Muslims gather for a Ramadan meal at the Islamic Center of America in Detroit, in December 2001.

Looking Ahead

For eight hundred years, Muslims led the world in science and learning, in making new inventions, and in travel and trade. Then the Muslim countries lost their power and were colonized or occupied by Western nations. Many Muslims are still angry about this and have tried to make Islam stronger by following the teachings of Islam more strictly. Other Muslims feel it was their own fault that they lost power, and they are eager to build links with the West and to live according to the will of God—in peace with the rest of the world.

In Our Own Words

"I'm proud to be Muslim. I cover my head, I grow a beard like all proper Muslim men should. I don't wear Western clothes, and I've got satellite television, so I need only watch Arabic programs. My duty as a Muslim is to fight for God—even if he wants me to give up my life. What's wrong with that?"

Glossary

Allah the Arabic word for God

ayatollah a leader of Shiite Muslims

Bismillah the words that open every chapter of the Koran (except the ninth): "In the name of Allah, the compassionate, the merciful"

calligraphy the art of beautiful handwriting

cremation the burning of a body after death

crusade a medieval Christian war against Muslims

Exordium the opening words of the Koran

Hadith the sayings of the Prophet Muhammad

hafiz the title given to a person who has learned the Koran by heart

Hajj the annual journey or pilgrimage to Mecca

hijab a veil that covers the head and shoulders, worn by some Muslim women

Hijrah the departure of the Prophet from Mecca for Yathrib (Medina, or Al-Madinah, Saudi Arabia) in 622 C.E., the date from which Islamic years are counted

id (*eid*) a festival

idol a statue or image worshiped as a god

iftar food eaten at the end of the day's fast during Ramadan

ilm the pursuit of knowledge and learning

imam a Muslim (man) who leads prayers in a mosque

Islam the Muslim faith; means literally "peace and submission" or "obedience to God"

Kaaba the cube-like structure in the center of the Great Mosque in Mecca, believed to be the first house built (by Adam) for the worship of the one true God

khalifah ("successor") one of the early leaders of Islam

mihrab an arch in a mosque, showing the direction of Mecca and the Kaaba

minaret the tall tower of a mosque

mu'adhin (*muezzin*) a man who calls Muslims to prayer

Moguls the rulers of a powerful Muslim Empire in India. Founded in 1526, it eventually came to an end in 1858.

Muslim a follower of Islam

Ottomans rulers of a powerful Muslim empire based in present-day Turkey, with its capital at Istanbul. It lasted from about 1300 to 1920.

qiblah the direction in which Muslims face when praying, toward Mecca and the Kaaba

Koran (*Qur'an*) ("recitation") the Muslim holy book, revealed to the Prophet Muhammad

Ramadan the ninth month of the Muslim year, during which Muslims fast during daylight hours

rashidun the "rightly guided ones": the first four khalifahs, Abu Bakr, Umar, Uthman, and Ali

revelation a message from God

salah (*salat*) praying five times a day

sawm fasting from dawn to sunset during the month of Ramadan

Shahadah the summary of the most important Muslim belief: "There is no god but God, and Muhammad, peace be upon him, is his Prophet"

sharia (*shari'ah*) the "way" or "path" followed by all Muslims; religious/civil law based on the Koran and the Sunnah

Shiite (*Shi'ah*) Muslims who believe in the genetic or family successorship of the fourth khalifah, Ali, after the Prophet Muhammad and eleven other imams after him

Sirah a written account of all the activities of the Prophet Muhammad

soul the inner, spirit-like part of a person, said to live on forever

sufi Muslims who try to become close to God by leading very simple lives and by using techniques such as chanting and dancing

suhoor a light meal eaten before dawn during Ramadan

Sunnah ("method" or "example") the life, thoughts, and sayings of the Prophet; the Hadith plus the Sirah

Sunni Muslims who believe in successorship (based on ability, not family) of the rashidun, the first four khalifahs after the death of the Prophet Muhammad

surah a chapter of the Koran

Taliban the fundamentalist Muslim government that controlled Afghanistan from 1996 until 2001

tawhid the belief that there is one and only one true God; monotheism

wudu washing before prayer, before touching the Koran, or before entering a mosque

zakah (*zakat*) one of the five "pilars" of Islam; an annual gift of money or other offerings to the needy that is given as an act of worship and purification

Time Line

C.E.

c. 570	Birth of the Prophet Muhammad
595	The Prophet marries Khadijah
610	The Prophet receives the first revelations from the Angel Jibril
622	The Prophet makes the Hijrah to Medina; Muslim calendar dates from this year
630	Muhammad takes control of Mecca and throws idols out of the Kaaba
632	Death of the Prophet; Abu Bakr becomes first khalifah
634–44	Umar is second khalifah
638	Muslims conquer Jerusalem
644–56	Uthman bin Affan is third khalifah
656–61	Ali bin Talib is fourth khalifah
690s	Dome of the Rock mosque completed in Jerusalem
732	By this date, Muslim rule extends from Spain to India
762–66	Building of Baghdad, then the largest city on earth
1023–91	Abbasid Dynasty rules Spain
1099	Christian crusaders conquer Jerusalem
1187	Muslims under Salah-ad-Din retake the city of Jerusalem

1301	Founding of the Ottoman Empire
1501–1732	Safavid Empire
1520–1566	Reign of Emperor Suleiman
1526	Founding of Mogul Empire
1857	British capture Delhi, India
1858	End of the Mogul Empire
1918	Collapse of the Ottoman Empire
1926–1932	Establishment of the united kingdom of Saudi Arabia
1947	British rule ends in India, which is partitioned to form Muslim state of Pakistan
1964	Founding of the Palestine Liberation Organization (PLO)
1967	Israel defeats Arabs in the Six Day War
1968	PLO turns to terrorism
1979	Establishment of the Islamic Republic of Iran applies fundamentalist sharia laws
1982	President Anwar Sadat of Egypt assassinated by Islamic fundamentalists
1996–2001	Taliban rules Afghanistan
2001 Sept.	Al Qaeda terrorist attacks in New York City, Washington, D.C., and Pennsylania kill about 3,000
2001 Oct.	The United States and Britain launch war on Afghanistan and oust Taliban

Books

Elias, Jamal J. *Religions of the World: Islam.* Prentice Hall, 1998.

Feiler, Bruce. *Abraham: A Journey to the Heart of Three Faiths.* Harper Perennial (series). HarperCollins Publishers, 2004.

Fiscus, James W. *America's War in Afghanistan (War and Conflict in the Middle East).* Rosen Publishing Group, 2004.

King, Zelda. *The Story of Our Numbers: The History of Arabic Numerals.* Powermath (series). PowerKids Press, 2004.

Self, David. *World Religions.* Lion Publishing, 2001.

Woolf, Alex. *Ideas of the Modern World: Fundamentalism.* Raintree, 2003.

Web Sites

www.frickart.org/programs/exhibitions/detail/63.html

www.holidays.net/ramadan/story.htm

www.islam101.com/dawah/zakah.htm

www.IslamOnline.net/english/introducingislam/index.shtml

www.islamicart.com/main/calligraphy/intro.html

www.moonsighting.com/calendar.html

www.timeforkids.com/TFK/news/story/0,6260,184391,00.html

Index